#movements

#BlackLivesMatter

Protesting Racism

Rachael L. Thomas

Abdo & Daughters

An Imprint of Abdo Publishing
abdobooks.com

abdobooks.com

Published by Abdo Publishing, a division of ABDO, PO Box 398166,
Minneapolis, Minnesota 55439. Copyright © 2020 by Abdo Consulting
Group, Inc. International copyrights reserved in all countries. No part of this
book may be reproduced in any form without written permission from the
publisher. Abdo & Daughters™ is a trademark and logo of Abdo Publishing.

Printed in the United States of America, North Mankato, Minnesota
052019
092019

THIS BOOK CONTAINS
RECYCLED MATERIALS

Design: Aruna Rangarajan, Mighty Media, Inc.
Production: Mighty Media, Inc.
Editor: Liz Salzmann
Cover Photographs: Shutterstock
Interior Photographs: Design elements, Shutterstock; Aamatos/Wikimedia
    Commons, pp. 17, 29 (top); Alamy, pp. 12–13; AP Images, pp. 4–5, 11, 19,
    22–23, 29 (bottom); courtesy of Dr. Eduardo Bonilla-Silva, p. 24; Everett
    Collection, p. 9; iStockphoto, pp. 26–27; Shutterstock, pp. 3, 6–7, 15, 20, 21,
    28 (top), 28 (bottom)

Library of Congress Control Number: 2018966471

Publisher's Cataloging-in-Publication Data
Names: Thomas, Rachael L., author.
Title: #BlackLivesMatter: protesting racism / by Rachael L. Thomas
Other title: Protesting racism
Description: Minneapolis, Minnesota : Abdo Publishing, 2020 | Series:
    #Movements | Includes online resources and index.
Identifiers: ISBN 9781532119293 (lib. bdg.) | ISBN 9781532173752 (ebook)
Subjects: LCSH: Black lives matter movement--Juvenile literature. | African
    Americans--Civil rights.--Juvenile literature. | Racial profiling in law
    enforcement--United States.--Juvenile literature. | Protest movements--
    Juvenile literature.
Classification: DDC 361.1--dc23

CONTENTS

It was February 26, 2012. Trayvon Martin, a young black teenager in Sanford, Florida, had been visiting his father. As Martin was walking home that night, he was spotted by neighborhood watch member George Zimmerman.

Zimmerman was sitting in his car when he saw Martin walking. Zimmerman thought Martin seemed suspicious. So, he called 911 to report Martin. The 911 operator told Zimmerman to stay in his car and wait for the police. However, he decided to get out of his car and follow Martin.

Zimmerman and Martin had a confrontation. In the struggle, Zimmerman shot Martin dead. Zimmerman said that Martin started the fight, and Zimmerman acted in self-defense. However, Martin was unarmed, so many people didn't believe Zimmerman. Some also thought Zimmerman initially followed Martin because Martin was black. They felt the shooting was racially motivated.

In April 2012, Zimmerman was charged with the murder of Martin. People around the country closely followed the trial. In July 2013, Zimmerman was acquitted of Martin's murder. Many black Americans saw the acquittal as evidence of racism in the US. It sparked fury in many people who felt the law did not protect black Americans as it should.

Martin was wearing a hooded sweatshirt when he was shot. Because of this, a demonstration in New York City was called the Million Hoodie March. Martin's parents, Tracy Martin (*center*) and Sybrina Fulton (*right*), attended the event.

After Zimmerman's acquittal, a new hashtag appeared on social media. It spread quickly across all social media services. Americans were telling the world that #BlackLivesMatter.

Racism toward black people in the US dates back to colonial times. During the 1600s and 1700s, the economy in the American colonies grew rapidly. This was due to the sale of crops such as tobacco.

But this economic growth had a negative side. Millions of people were abducted from the African continent and brought across the Atlantic Ocean. They were made to work as slaves on plantations that grew tobacco and other crops. These slaves were considered property. Owners bought and sold slaves, often separating members of families. Slaves were also often physically abused by their owners.

People in the northern states were less in favor of slavery than those in the South. By 1804, slavery was abolished in all northern states. But southern states, where most plantations were located, continued to allow slavery.

LET'S TALK TERMS

Racism is the belief that one race is better than another. In the US, white people have historically had more social and economic power than people of other races. So, racism in the US is generally considered to be directed toward non-white people.

6

Africans were brought to North and South America in slave ships. More than ten million people were shipped across the ocean between the 1500s and 1800s.

Over the next fifty years, tension over slavery would divide the country. This was a major issue that led to the American Civil War.

In 1865, the northern states won the Civil War and Congress passed the Thirteenth Amendment. This Amendment abolished slavery. Millions of African Americans were ready to rebuild their lives as free people.

Slavery was made illegal across the US in 1865. But the rights of African Americans were slow to improve. In the South especially, racism was widespread. Organizations such as the Ku Klux Klan were formed. The Ku Klux Klan is a white supremacist group. This means it believes white people deserve more rights than people of all other races. Members of white supremacist groups often acted with violence toward black people.

In the 1870s and 1880s, some states passed laws called "Jim Crow" laws. Jim Crow laws were intended to keep blacks and whites separate. For example, white and black students went to separate schools. And black people had to sit in separate areas of buses and trains. This is called segregation.

Jim Crow laws were maintained for a century. In 1964, President Lyndon B. Johnson signed the Civil Rights Act. This was an important milestone in the history of civil rights in America. The act made Jim Crow laws and other segregation policies illegal.

Discrimination based on skin color remains illegal today. But attitudes change more slowly than laws. Fifty years after the Civil Rights Act, many black Americans were still experiencing discrimination. And the shooting of Martin in 2012 marked the start of a national discussion about racial bias, especially among law enforcement officials.

The US Supreme Court officially ended school segregation in May 1954. Some states allowed black and white students to attend the same schools that fall. Other states fought the ruling and took many years to desegregate their schools.

A Hashtag Is Born

Trayvon Martin was shot and killed by George Zimmerman in February 2012. Three weeks later, an investigation was launched into Martin's death. The investigation and trial took longer than a year. On July 13, 2013, the jury declared George Zimmerman not guilty.

Civil rights activist Alicia Garza was one of many around the country awaiting the verdict. After the acquittal of George Zimmerman, Garza posted a message on Facebook. She expressed her love for black people. She asked that they come together to declare that black lives matter. Hundreds of thousands of people of all races would do just that.

Activist Patrisse Cullors created the hashtag #BlackLivesMatter in July 2013. By July 2014, the hashtag was being used an average of 48 times per day. However, this number was small compared to what it would become.

Use of the #BlackLivesMatter hashtag increased dramatically after the shooting of Michael Brown in August 2014. Michael Brown was an 18-year-old black teenager from Ferguson, Missouri. On August 9, 2014, he was shot dead by white police officer Darren Wilson.

That morning, Brown was walking with a friend. Wilson stopped them because Brown fit the description of a robbery suspect. Wilson claimed that he shot Brown in self-defense as Brown ran toward him.

THE FACES OF #BLM

Founders Garza, Cullors, and Tometi

Alicia Garza, Patrisse Cullors, and Opal Tometi are African American women from San Francisco, Los Angeles, and New York. In 2012, the three women were all working to promote and organize black activism in their cities.

The day after Zimmerman's acquittal, Garza wrote a Facebook post saying, "Black people. I love you. I love us. Our lives matter." Cullors saw Garza's post and responded with similar posts on her own social media accounts. She created the hashtag #BlackLivesMatter.

Tometi was moved by Cullors's and Garza's posts. She reached out to the two women. Tometi offered to build and manage social media accounts to support what Garza and Cullors had started.

"Black Lives Matter is our call to action. It is about replacing narratives of Black criminality with Black humanity."
—Patrisse Cullors

(left to right) Garza, Cullors, Tometi

However, witness accounts of the event varied. Some witnesses recounted the events differently from how Wilson reported them.

Because of the varying statements, the actual events that led to Brown's shooting are uncertain. But because Brown had been unarmed, his shooting sparked protests across Ferguson. Hundreds of people took to the streets. Ferguson police used tear gas, rubber bullets, and pepper spray to subdue protesters.

The St. Louis County prosecutor formed a grand jury to decide whether to charge Wilson with a crime for shooting Brown. On November 24, the grand jury voted against this action. So, Wilson was not charged for Brown's death.

The #BlackLivesMatter hashtag suddenly exploded across social media. In the 20 hours before the grand jury's decision, the hashtag was used 10,000 times. In the four hours that followed the verdict, it was used a total of 92,784 times. #BlackLivesMatter had officially become a call for change across the US.

A common theme of the Brown protests was "hands up, don't shoot." This was because according to some accounts, Brown had his hands in the air when he was shot.

Black Lives Matter Global Network

The #BlackLivesMatter hashtag brought the phrase into the public eye. In 2014, the hashtag grew into an official organization. The organization promotes activism in black communities. Its full name is the Black Lives Matter Global Network (BLM).

BLM's mission is to stop the violence suffered by black communities. But it is also a movement marked by modern-day lifestyles and values. For example, civil rights movements have historically been led by one or a few main leaders. BLM is different.

BLM encourages equal leadership and involvement from all of its members. This is because BLM founders want the movement to represent every type of black American. This includes gay, transgender, and disabled people. And many white Americans, Hispanic Americans, and Asian Americans are involved in the Black Lives Matter movement as well.

BLM was born in defiance of police violence. But today, founder Alicia Garza worries that the wider message BLM carries is sometimes lost. Garza says, "…what black folks are fighting for in this moment…isn't citizenship like papers, but it's citizenship like dignity."

Specific centers for BLM activism are called chapters. As of January 2019, there were 24 BLM chapters in the US.

The Ripple Effect

The Black Lives Matter movement has empowered black communities to stand up to violence and discrimination. It has also been recognized as a national force for change. In August 2015, key figures in the Black Lives Matter movement created an initiative called Campaign Zero.

Campaign Zero aims to improve police conduct. It suggests changes to police policy. These suggestions include increased use of body cameras and better training for officers. Body cameras record police interactions with citizens. These recordings can help identify when police officers are acting on bias or with unnecessary violence. Police training suggestions include practicing how to resolve conflicts without violence. As of 2018, 40 US states have passed laws to address at least one Campaign Zero policy suggestion.

Individuals have also started independent projects to strive for fairness. Samuel Sinyangwe is a data analyst who grew up near where Martin was shot. After the Michael Brown shooting, he tried to research US deaths caused by police. He wanted to know where fatal incidents were occurring and who the victims were.

Sinyangwe found this search difficult. He discovered that there wasn't a federal database tracking information about police shootings. So, there weren't accurate records of people killed by police officers in the US.

Sinyangwe helped form the group We The Protestors. This organization develops digital tools to support the work of Black Lives Matter.

Sinyangwe used a number of online databases to gather information on police killings. Then, he founded the website mappingpoliceviolence.org and published his findings. The website aims to provide accurate information about police violence in the US. Projects like Campaign Zero and Mapping Police Violence can help hold police officers responsible for the deaths of civilians.

Three years after #BlackLivesMatter was born, the conversation about police behavior continued. Videos of police officers shooting unarmed black civilians had gone viral. More and more people were questioning how black communities were treated by law enforcement.

On August 26, 2016, the National Football League (NFL) became part of this conversation. The San Francisco 49ers had a pre-season home game against the Green Bay Packers. When the national anthem played before the game, 49ers quarterback Colin Kaepernick did not stand. Instead, he remained seated on the players' bench. The next week, he started kneeling during the anthem before each game.

TAGGED

"Don't confuse #TakeAKnee for disrespect. Respect and love for America doesn't require blindness to its failures."
—New York Civil Liberties Union (@NYCLU, Twitter)

The US national anthem is played before all NFL games. Usually, people stand for the anthem. It is considered a gesture of respect and pride for one's country. But Kaepernick knelt to show his support for the Black Lives Matter movement. Kaepernick said he was not willing to show pride in his country while it oppressed its black citizens.

Fellow San Francisco 49ers player Eric Reid (*left*) often knelt with Kaepernick (*right*) during the national anthem.

In the two weeks following the August 26 game, Kaepernick gained almost 100,000 new Twitter followers. This was more than twice the number of followers he had gained over the previous eight months! A new hashtag, #TakeAKnee, emerged from Kaepernick's protest.

Over following NFL seasons, the #TakeAKnee movement continued to grow. More and more football players began to kneel during the US national anthem. Kaepernick became a symbol of protest and change.

Kaepernick has become widely respected for using his fame to raise awareness of the oppression of black Americans. But the #TakeAKnee movement has inspired opposition as well as support. Those against the gesture accuse Kaepernick of being disrespectful and unpatriotic. However, supporters believe Kaepernick's protest is patriotic because its goal is to better the country.

Some people joined the #TakeAKnee movement to honor black men, such as Philando Castile, who had been killed by police officers.

THE FACE OF #TAKEAKNEE

Colin Kaepernick

Colin Kaepernick played for the San Francisco 49ers from 2011 to 2016. In August 2016, he sat during a pre-game national anthem to protest the treatment of black Americans. This sparked the creation of the hashtag #TakeAKnee.

Kaepernick is highly involved in his community. In 2016, he founded the youth camp Know Your Rights. The camp teaches young people empowerment, motivation, and how to interact with law enforcement. Kaepernick also pledged to give $1 million to organizations fighting for social justice. He fulfilled this Million Dollar Pledge in January 2018.

"I am not going to stand up to show pride in a flag for a country that oppresses black people and people of color. To me, this is bigger than football, and it would be selfish on my part to look the other way."
—Colin Kaepernick

While #TakeAKnee was just getting started, #BlackLivesMatter was still going strong. In November 2017, BLM was awarded the Sydney Peace Prize. A former professor from the University of Sydney in Australia established the Sydney Peace Foundation and the award in 1998. The award's purpose is to recognize people who work for peace, human rights, or social justice. The year 2017 was the first that an organization, rather than an individual, received the award. The Sydney Peace Foundation congratulated BLM for creating "a unique opportunity to change the course of history."

But not all reactions to Black Lives Matter were positive. Critics have suggested that the movement favors the lives of black people over white people. This belief led to the creation of the hashtag #AllLivesMatter.

Some critics also disliked that BLM's mission challenges the behavior of police officers. They argued that the risks police officers face were being overlooked by BLM. People also pointed out that police officers are sometimes killed, not just black civilians. This objection resulted in the hashtag #BlueLivesMatter. This hashtag refers to the blue uniforms that US police officers often wear.

In July 2017, supporters of the New York Police Department used the #BlueLivesMatter hashtag in memory of officers killed in the line of duty.

24

BLM founder Garza argues that both reactions miss the point. She calls the fact that all lives matter "obvious." She points out that the values of police officers' lives and, more generally, white Americans' lives, have never been in question. Black people, on the other hand, have been battling for many decades to be seen as equals.

Some researchers believe the backlash against BLM is due in part to differing perceptions of racism. Sociologist Eduardo Bonilla-Silva explains these differences in his book *Racism without Racists*. He says that white people often perceive racism as being a past problem, separate from their current behaviors and communities. They consider racist people to be exceptions in an otherwise non-racist society.

Bonilla-Silva says that African Americans tend to view racism differently. Most see racism as a part of society. Many black Americans believe that racism is deeply established in US history, law, and culture.

BLM wants to address these different perceptions of racism. It claims that it does not represent a war that divides the country. In fact, people of all races are committed to the goals of BLM.

BLM supporters say that declaring "black lives matter" does not suggest other lives matter less. Rather, it is a way to expose and solve the problems that black communities face. To do so, supporters say people must first acknowledge these problems.

Bonilla-Silva is a sociology professor at Duke University and a former president of the American Sociological Association.

Black Lives Matter is an example of a force for change that was amplified by social media. As of July 2018, the hashtag #BlackLivesMatter had been used on Twitter more than 30 million times. That's an average of 17,000 times per day!

#BlackLivesMatter brought thousands of people together. It sparked an important conversation about race in America. Policy changes driven by the movement have changed US law enforcement for the better.

Meanwhile, BLM's founders continue working to amplify African American voices and influence. In January 2018, Cullors published *When They Call You a Terrorist: A Black Lives Matter Memoir*. In the book, she writes about how her experiences led her to work for civil rights.

In February 2018, Garza launched Black Futures Lab. This organization aims to build black power in politics. Black Futures Lab programs include the Black Census Project. Through this project, organizers interview members of the African American community to learn about their experiences and goals. This information will help shape policies that affect black communities.

Those involved in the Black Lives Matter movement say there is much more to be done. But with the help of social media, Black Lives Matter has continued forging the path toward racial justice and equality.

#BlackLivesMatter is the modern face of the decades-long fight for dignity, equality, and civil rights.

#BLACK LIVES MATTER

LO, 1995
RAY, 2013
LDADE, 2012
THY RUSSELL, 2012
ERSON, 2012
003
RY JR.,
2004

LAQUAN MCDONALD, 2014

VONDERRIT MYERS JR, 2
KAREN CIFUENTES, 2014
DIANA SHOWMAN, 2014
ROSHAD MCINTOSH, 20
ERIC MICHAEL GARNE 20
BROWN, 2014
JOHN CRAWFO

TIMELINE

Black teenager Trayvon Martin is shot dead in Sanford, Florida, by neighborhood watch member George Zimmerman.

Black Lives Matter Global Network is established.

February 2012

2014

July 2013

August 2014

Black Lives Matter founder Patrisse Cullors creates the hashtag #BlackLivesMatter. Zimmerman is acquitted of Trayvon Martin's murder.

Michael Brown, a black teenager from Ferguson, Missouri, is shot dead.

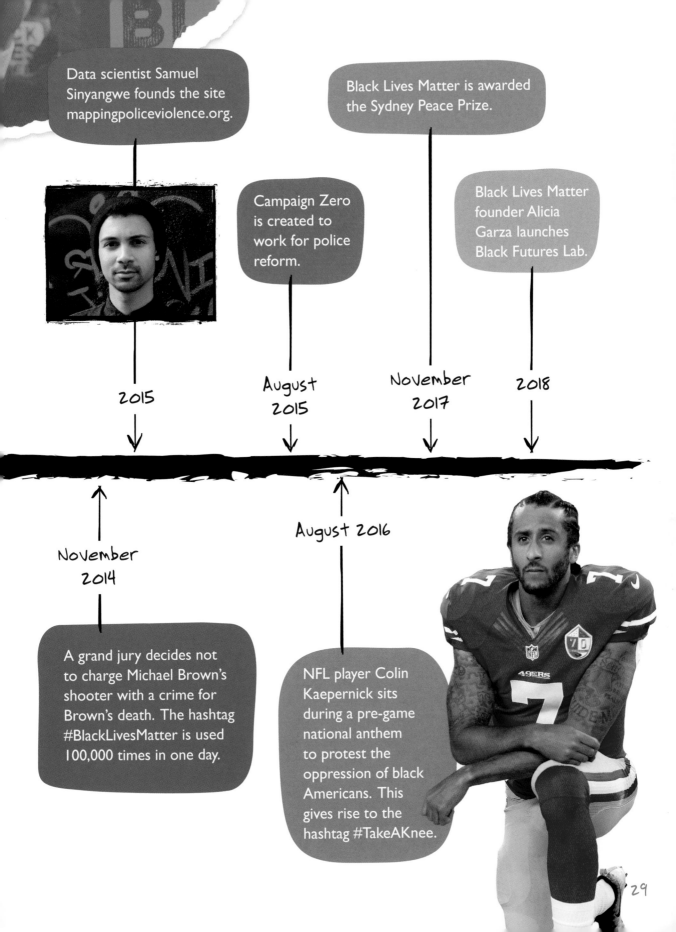

Data scientist Samuel Sinyangwe founds the site mappingpoliceviolence.org.

Black Lives Matter is awarded the Sydney Peace Prize.

Campaign Zero is created to work for police reform.

Black Lives Matter founder Alicia Garza launches Black Futures Lab.

2015

August 2015

November 2017

2018

November 2014

August 2016

A grand jury decides not to charge Michael Brown's shooter with a crime for Brown's death. The hashtag #BlackLivesMatter is used 100,000 times in one day.

NFL player Colin Kaepernick sits during a pre-game national anthem to protest the oppression of black Americans. This gives rise to the hashtag #TakeAKnee.

29

GLOSSARY

activism—a practice that emphasizes direct action in support of or in opposition to an issue that causes disagreement. A person who practices activism is an activist.

amendment—a change to a country's or a state's constitution.

analyst—a person who determines the meaning of something by breaking down its parts.

anthem—a song of gladness or patriotism.

backlash—a strong public reaction against something.

Civil War—the war between the United States of America and the Confederate States of America from 1861 to 1865.

civilian—a person who is not an active member of a police force or the military.

dignity—the quality of being respected or worthy.

discrimination—unfair treatment, often based on race, religion, or gender.

empower—to help people gain control over their own lives. This process is called empowerment.

grand jury—a group of people who review evidence against someone who has been accused of a crime and decide if the person should be tried in court.

hashtag—a word or phrase used in social media posts, such as tweets, that starts with the symbol # and that briefly indicates what the post is about.

neighborhood watch—a group of volunteers who look out for criminal activity in their community and call the police when they see something suspicious.

prosecutor—a lawyer who represents the government in court cases.

segregation—the separation of an individual or a group from a larger group, especially by race.

social media—websites or smartphone apps that provide information and entertainment and allow people to communicate with each other. Facebook and Twitter are examples of social media.

viral—quickly or widely spread, usually by electronic communication.

white supremacist—a person who believes that the white race is better than all other races and should have more power and privileges than other races.

ONLINE RESOURCES

Booklinks
NONFICTION NETWORK
FREE! ONLINE NONFICTION RESOURCES

To learn more about #BlackLivesMatter, please visit **abdobooklinks.com** or scan this QR code. These links are routinely monitored and updated to provide the most current information available.

INDEX